MathFlare

Name: ________________________

Class: ___________

Teacher: ________________________

Introduction

As parents and educators, we recognize the pivotal role mathematics plays in shaping a child's academic journey and future success. Yet, the path to mathematical proficiency can often seem daunting, fraught with challenges and complexities. That's where the transformative power of MathFlare Workbooks shine through, illuminating the way forward with clarity, precision, and purpose.

Introducing MathFlare Workbooks – a beacon of guidance, a testament to excellence, and a catalyst for achievement. Crafted with meticulous care and expertise, MathFlare Workbooks stand as paragons of educational excellence, designed to nurture young minds, ignite a passion for learning, and develop a deep-rooted understanding of mathematical concepts.

Picture this: your child eagerly delves into the pages of Mathflare Workbook, greeted by a step-by-step guide illuminated with vivid examples that demystify complex mathematical concepts. With each turn of the page, they embark on a journey of discovery, encountering thoughtfully curated practice questions that reinforce learning and hone problem-solving skills. And when they unveil the answers to those very questions, a sense of accomplishment blossoms within them – a tangible reward for their hard work and dedication.

But MathFlare Workbooks are more than just tools for learning; they are pathways to comprehension, fostering a deep-seated understanding of mathematical concepts through a sequential, logical flow. From fundamental principles to advanced problem-solving strategies, every chapter builds upon the last, ensuring a robust foundation upon which future knowledge can be constructed.

As parents, we yearn for nothing more than to see our children thrive, to witness the spark of inspiration ignited within them as they conquer academic challenges with confidence and poise. MathFlare Workbooks serve as partners in this noble endeavor, offering not just practice questions, but the keys to unlocking a world of opportunity.

And for teachers, MathFlare Workbooks stand as invaluable allies in the quest to cultivate mathematical proficiency in the classroom. With answers readily available, instructors can focus on guiding and nurturing their students, confident in the knowledge that MathFlare Workbooks provide a solid framework upon which to build.

In the pages of MathFlare Workbooks, we find not just the promise of academic excellence, but the seeds of a brighter tomorrow. So let us embrace the power of mathematics, let us champion the journey of learning, and let us pave the way for a generation of young minds poised to shape the world. With MathFlare Workbooks as our guide, the possibilities are infinite, and the future, bright.

Table of Contents

MathFlare
MATH WORKBOOK
Grade 2
Step by Step Guide and Essential Practice with Answers
Addition Subtraction
Multiplication
Place Value and Expanded Notations
Geometry
MathFlare Publishing

MathFlare
MATH WORKBOOK
Grade 2-3
Step by Step Guide and Essential Practice with Answers
Addition Subtraction
Multiplication and Division
Place Value and Expanded Notations
Geometry
MathFlare Publishing

MathFlare
MATH WORKBOOK
Grade 3
Step by Step Guide and Essential Practice with Answers
Multiplication and Division
Decimals
Place Value and Expanded Notations
Fractions and Geometry
MathFlare Publishing

MathFlare
MATH WORKBOOK
Grade 1
Step by Step Guide and Essential Practice with Answers
Counting and Numbers
Addition and Subtraction
Place Value and Expanded Notations
Understanding Time
MathFlare Publishing

MathFlare
MATH WORKBOOK
Grade 1-2
Step by Step Guide and Essential Practice with Answers
Counting and Numbers
Addition and Subtraction
Place Value and Expanded Notations
Understanding Time
MathFlare Publishing

MathFlare
MATH WORKBOOK
Grade 3-4
Step by Step Guide and Essential Practice with Answers
Addition Subtraction
Multiplication Division
Place Value and Expanded Notations
Fractions and Geometry
MathFlare Publishing

MathFlare
MATH WORKBOOK
Grade 4
Step by Step Guide and Essential Practice with Answers
Addition Subtraction
Multiplication Division
Place Value and Expanded Notations
Fractions and Geometry
MathFlare Publishing

MathFlare
MATH WORKBOOK
Grade 4-5
Step by Step Guide and Essential Practice with Answers
Multiplication Division
Place Value and Expanded Notations
Fractions and Geometry
Unit Conversion
MathFlare Publishing

MathFlare
MATH
WORKBOOK
Grade 5
Step by Step Guide
and Essential Practice
with Answers
Multiplication
Division
Place Value and
Expanded Notations
Fractions
and Geometry
Unit Conversion
MathFlare Publishing

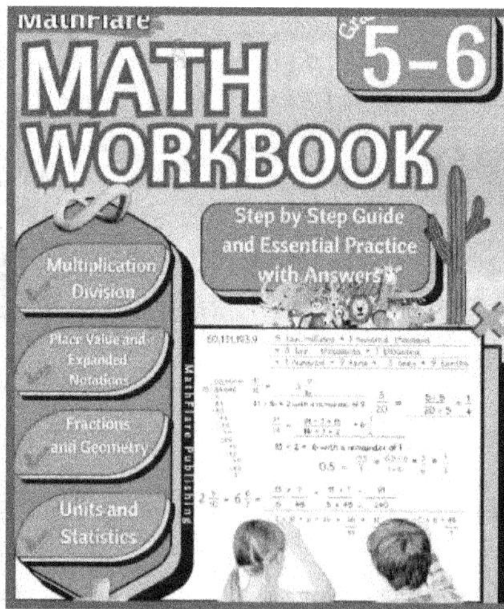
MathFlare
MATH
WORKBOOK
Grade 5-6
Step by Step Guide
and Essential Practice
with Answers
Multiplication
Division
Place Value and
Expanded Notations
Fractions
and Geometry
Units and
Statistics
MathFlare Publishing

MathFlare
MATH
WORKBOOK
Grade 6
Step by Step Guide
and Essential Practice
with Answers
Integers and
Statistics
Arithmetic and
Pre-Algebra
Fractions
and Geometry
Ratio and
Percentage
MathFlare Publishing

MathFlare
MATH
WORKBOOK
Grade 6-7
Step by Step Guide
and Essential Practice
with Answers
Arithmetic and
Pre-Algebra
Ratio, Percent
Proportion
Geometry
Statistics
MathFlare Publishing

MathFlare
MATH
WORKBOOK
Grade 7
Step by Step Guide
and Essential Practice
with Answers
Pre-Algebra
Ratio, Percent
Proportion
Geometry
Statistics
MathFlare Publishing

MathFlare
MATH
WORKBOOK
Grade 7-8
Step by Step Guide
and Essential Practice
with Answers
Pre-Algebra
Ratio, Percent
Proportion
Geometry and
Cartesian Plane
Statistics
MathFlare Publishing

MathFlare
MATH
WORKBOOK
Grade 8-9
Step by Step Guide
and Essential Practice
with Answers
Pre-Algebra
Ratio, Proportion
and Percentage
Linear Equations
Geometry and
Cartesian Plane
MathFlare Publishing

MathFlare
MATH
WORKBOOK
Grade 8
Step by Step Guide
and Essential Practice
with Answers
Pre-Algebra
Percentage
Linear Equations
Geometry
MathFlare Publishing

Place Value and Expanded Notations

Place value tells us the value of a digit in a number based on where it's placed.

Imagine we have the number 35,987,647.52843. It has 13 digits.

Now, each digit holds a special place. Let's break down the number 35,987,647.52843:

- The digit 3 is in the ten millions place. Its value is 3 × 1,000,000=30,000,000.

- The digit 5 is in the millions place. Its value is 5 × 1,000,000=5,000,000.

- The digit 9 is in the hundred thousands place. Its value is 9×100,000=900,000.

- The digit 8 is in the ten thousands place. Its value is 8×10,000=80,000.

- The digit 7 is in the thousands place. Its value is 7×1,000=7,000.

- The digit 6 is in the hundreds place. Its value is 6×100=600.

- The digit 4 is in the tens place. Its value is 4×10=40.

- The digit 7 is in the ones place. Its value is 7×1=7.

- The digit 5 is in the tenths place. Its value is $5 \times \frac{1}{10} = 0.5$.

- The digit 2 is in the hundredths place. Its value is $2 \times \frac{1}{100} = 0.02$.

- The digit 8 is in the thousandths place. Its value is $8 \times \frac{1}{1000} = 0.008$.

- The digit 4 is in the ten thousandths place. Its value is $4 \times \frac{1}{10,000} = 0.0004$.

- The digit 3 is in the hundred thousandths place. Its value is $3 \times \dfrac{1}{100,000} =$ 0.00003.

When we add these values together, we find the value of the entire number:

$$30,000,000 + 5,000,000 + 900,000 + 80,000 + 7,000 + 600 + 40 + 7 + 0.5 + 0.02$$
$$+ 0.008 + 0.0004 + 0.00003 = 35,987,647.52843$$

Let's solve some problems:

Place value of the underlined digit:

$$49,477,31\underline{3}.593 = \underline{\quad 3 \text{ ones} \quad}$$

Expanded notations:

86,951,328.0	8 ten millions + 6 millions + 9 hundred thousands + 5 ten thousands + 1 thousand + 3 hundreds + 2 tens + 8 ones
2,897,917.886	2,000,000 + 800,000 + 90,000 + 7,000 + 900 + 10 + 7 + 0.8 + 0.08 + 0.006

614,537,541.1   6 hundred millions + 1 ten million + 4 millions
+ 5 hundred thousands + 3 ten thousands
+ 7 thousands + 5 hundreds + 4 tens
+ 1 one + 1 tenth

Rounding Numbers

Rounding numbers is the process of approximating a numerical value to a certain degree of accuracy by replacing it with a simpler or more convenient value. Rounding is commonly used to simplify calculations and express numbers in a more manageable form.

Steps to Rounding Numbers:

1. **Identify the digit to be rounded:** Determine the digit to which the number will be rounded.

2. **Look at the next digit:** Examine the digit immediately to the right of the one being rounded.

3. **Decide whether to round up or down:** If the next digit is 5 or greater, round the digit up. If it is less than 5, round the digit down.

4. **Adjust the number:** Change the digit being rounded and replace all digits to the right with zeros if necessary.

Properties of Rounding Numbers:
1. **Accuracy:** Rounding reduces the precision of a number but maintains its approximate value.

2. **Simplicity:** Rounding simplifies calculations by using fewer digits.

3. **Ease of Use:** Rounding makes numbers easier to work with, especially in mental arithmetic and estimation.

Methods of Rounding Numbers:

1. **Round to Nearest Integer:** Round to the nearest whole number.

    I.   Round Up (Ceiling): Always round up to the nearest integer.

    II. Round Down (Floor): Always round down to the nearest integer.

2. **Round to Nearest Tenth:** Round to the nearest tenth (one decimal place).

3. **Round to Nearest Hundredth:** Round to the nearest hundredth (two decimal places).

4. **Round to Nearest Thousandth:** Round to the nearest thousandth (three decimal places).

5. **Round to Specific Decimal Places:** Round to a specified number of decimal places as needed.

Let's round the number **438,576.214** to various degrees of accuracy:

Rounding Level	Rounded Number	Difference from Original
Nearest Whole Number	438,576	0
Nearest Ten	438,580	+4
Nearest Hundred	438,600	+24
Nearest Thousand	439,000	+424
Nearest Ten Thousand	440,000	+3,424
Nearest Hundred Thousand	400,000	−38,576
Nearest Million	0.4386×10^6	−438,576.214

Place Value

Determine the place value of the underlined digit.

1. 821,6̲00,968.418 = _______________________________

2. 191,046,6̲30.435 = _______________________________

3. 403,48̲2,149.695 = _______________________________

4. 65̲4,815,300.055 = _______________________________

5. 834,319,7̲35.35 = _______________________________

6. 91̲2,763,731.708 = _______________________________

7. 390,935,265.00̲3 = _______________________________

Name:_________________   Date: ____________

8. 117,944,975.4<u>3</u>4 = _______________________________

9. 644,<u>9</u>89,197.059 = _______________________________

10. <u>2</u>58,367,068.887 = _______________________________

11. 652,971,<u>7</u>00.032 = _______________________________

12. 132,976,93<u>9</u>.352 = _______________________________

13. 197,123,<u>0</u>15.285 = _______________________________

14. 944,469,626.5<u>9</u>9 = _______________________________

15. 391,810,<u>5</u>82.542 = _______________________________

16. 537,480,337.05 = _______________________________

17. 984,607,850.614 = _______________________________

18. 227,642,511.294 = _______________________________

19. 280,544,026.492 = _______________________________

20. 873,708,026.297 = _______________________________

21. 485,267,554.035 = _______________________________

22. 133,099,450.506 = _______________________________

23. 524,519,648.275 = _______________________________

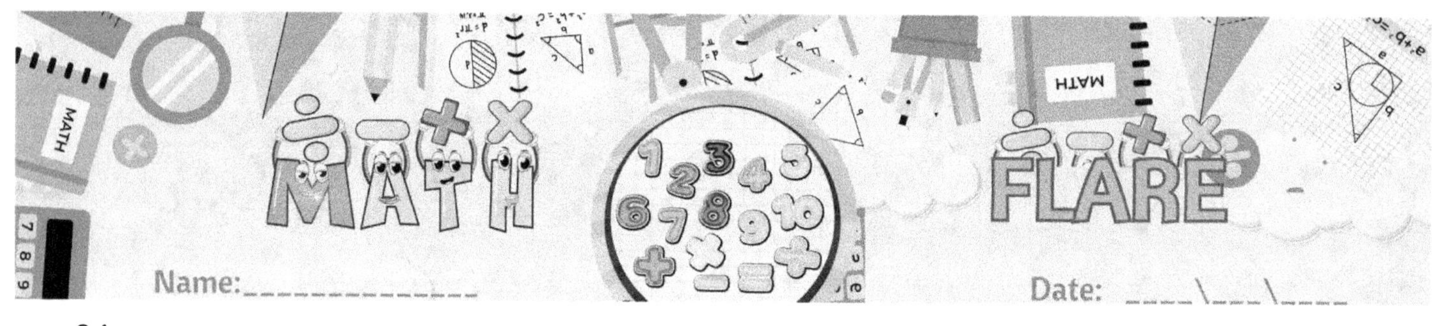

24. 710,688,075.037 = _______________________________

25. 383,908,974.573 = _______________________________

26. 569,457,303.109 = _______________________________

27. 199,683,549.242 = _______________________________

28. 883,164,106.825 = _______________________________

29. 545,894,822.777 = _______________________________

30. 441,486,706.613 = _______________________________

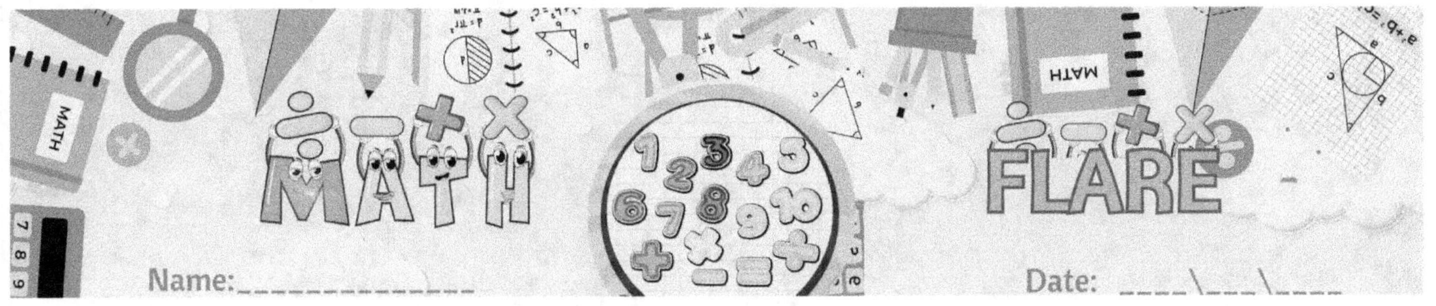

Place Value: Expanded Notation

Provide the expanded notation for each value.

31. _________________________________

1 million + 5 hundred thousands + 9 ten thousands + 6 thousands + 4 hundreds + 4 tens + 1 one + 9 tenths + 3 hundredths

32. _________________________________

9 millions + 6 hundred thousands + 3 ten thousands + 8 thousands + 2 hundreds + 6 tens + 9 ones + 7 tenths + 3 hundredths + 5 thousandths

33. _________________________________

7 millions + 4 hundred thousands + 6 ten thousands + 6 thousands + 2 hundreds + 6 tens + 1 one + 1 tenth + 8 hundredths + 9 thousandths

34. _________________________________

7 millions + 9 hundred thousands + 4 ten thousands + 3 hundreds + 3 tens + 8 ones + 3 tenths + 2 hundredths + 6 thousandths

35. _______________________________ 2 millions + 1 hundred thousand
+ 1 ten thousand + 1 thousand +
7 hundreds + 4 tens + 5 ones +
4 hundredths + 7 thousandths

36. _______________________________ 1 million + 9 hundred thousands
+ 1 ten thousand + 4 thousands
+ 7 hundreds + 6 tens + 4 ones
+ 7 tenths + 1 hundredth + 9
thousandths

37. _______________________________ 8 millions + 8 hundred
thousands + 3 ten thousands +
3 thousands + 8 hundreds + 4
tens + 4 ones + 3 tenths + 3
hundredths

38. _______________________________ 2 millions + 6 hundred
thousands + 8 ten thousands +
9 thousands + 3 hundreds + 1
ten + 1 tenth + 2 thousandths

39. ____________________________ 1 million + 4 hundred thousands + 9 ten thousands + 6 thousands + 6 hundreds + 2 tens + 8 ones + 4 tenths + 2 hundredths + 1 thousandth

40. ____________________________ 3 millions + 4 hundred thousands + 2 ten thousands + 5 thousands + 6 hundreds + 2 tenths + 7 hundredths + 3 thousandths

41. ____________________________ 7 millions + 1 hundred thousand + 9 ten thousands + 3 thousands + 5 hundreds + 6 tens + 3 ones + 6 hundredths + 4 thousandths

42. ____________________________ 4 millions + 4 hundred thousands + 2 ten thousands + 5 thousands + 1 hundred + 1 ten + 1 one + 3 tenths + 3 hundredths + 1 thousandth

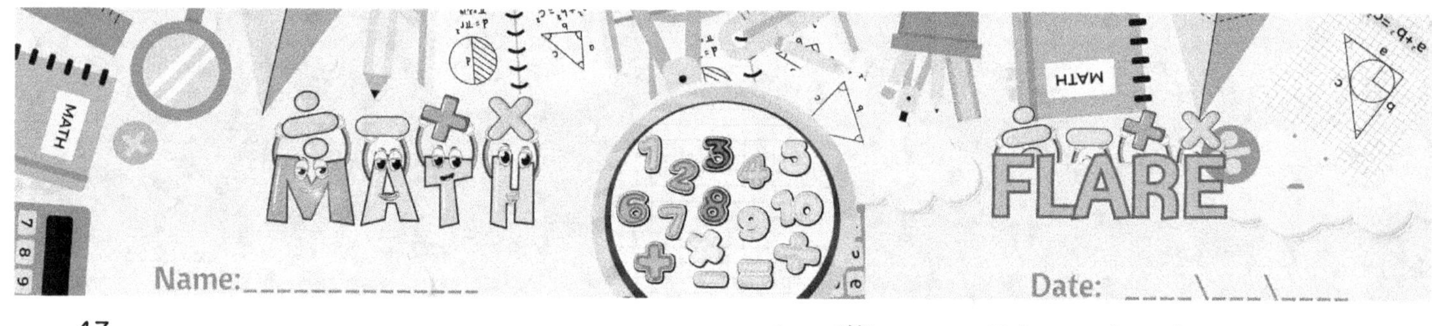

43. ______________________________

4 millions + 7 hundred thousands + 5 ten thousands + 9 thousands + 8 hundreds + 9 tens + 3 ones + 7 tenths + 6 hundredths + 4 thousandths

44. ______________________________

1 million + 3 hundred thousands + 2 ten thousands + 5 thousands + 9 hundreds + 1 ten + 1 one + 7 hundredths + 7 thousandths

45. ______________________________

3 millions + 3 hundred thousands + 1 ten thousand + 8 hundreds + 2 tens + 2 ones + 6 hundredths + 2 thousandths

46. ______________________________

8 millions + 3 hundred thousands + 7 ten thousands + 3 thousands + 8 tens + 4 ones + 5 thousandths

47. ________________________________ 4 millions + 3 hundred thousands + 9 ten thousands + 2 thousands + 1 hundred + 8 tens + 7 ones + 9 tenths + 5 hundredths + 7 thousandths

48. ________________________________ 2 millions + 4 hundred thousands + 3 ten thousands + 7 thousands + 7 hundreds + 7 ones + 4 tenths + 4 hundredths + 7 thousandths

49. ________________________________ 6 millions + 4 hundred thousands + 9 ten thousands + 7 thousands + 3 hundreds + 1 ten + 4 ones + 6 tenths + 7 hundredths + 4 thousandths

50. ________________________________ 5 millions + 7 hundred thousands + 9 thousands + 2 hundreds + 3 ones + 7 tenths + 5 thousandths

51. _________________________   7 millions + 5 hundred thousands + 1 ten thousand + 4 thousands + 2 hundreds + 7 tens + 9 ones + 9 tenths + 5 thousandths

52. _________________________   1 million + 3 ten thousands + 8 thousands + 1 hundred + 8 tens + 8 ones + 3 tenths + 2 hundredths + 8 thousandths

53. _________________________   3 millions + 7 ten thousands + 2 thousands + 3 hundreds + 7 tens + 2 ones + 2 tenths + 1 hundredth + 7 thousandths

54. _________________________   6 millions + 9 ten thousands + 1 hundred + 3 ones + 2 tenths + 5 hundredths + 2 thousandths

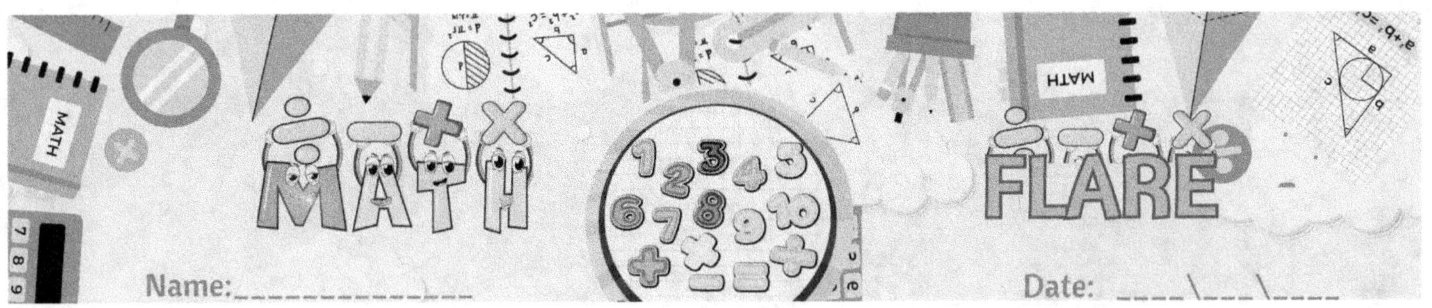

55. _________________________________

6 millions + 5 hundred thousands + 1 thousand + 6 hundreds + 5 tens + 9 ones + 2 tenths + 3 hundredths + 6 thousandths

56. _________________________________

6 millions + 4 hundred thousands + 5 ten thousands + 8 thousands + 3 hundreds + 2 tens + 1 one + 8 tenths + 4 hundredths + 2 thousandths

57. _________________________________

9 millions + 6 hundred thousands + 5 ten thousands + 5 thousands + 4 hundreds + 9 tens + 8 ones + 1 tenth

58. _________________________________

3 millions + 2 hundred thousands + 1 ten thousand + 9 hundreds + 4 tens + 1 one + 2 tenths + 8 thousandths

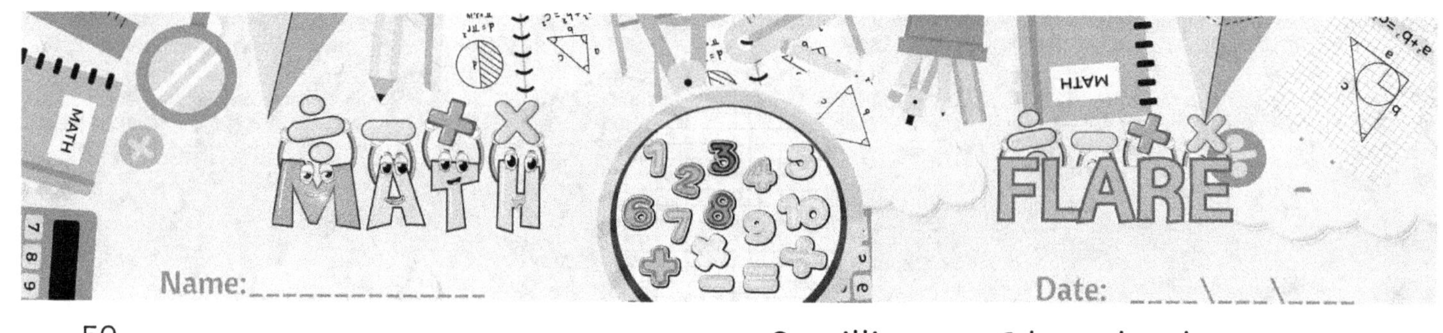

59. _______________________________ 2 millions + 6 hundred thousands + 4 ten thousands + 3 thousands + 4 hundreds + 2 tens + 1 one + 6 tenths + 1 hundredth + 3 thousandths

60. _______________________________ 1 million + 5 hundred thousands + 9 ten thousands + 9 thousands + 9 hundreds + 4 tens + 7 ones + 7 tenths + 6 hundredths + 6 thousandths

61. _______________________________ 5 millions + 6 hundred thousands + 9 ten thousands + 9 thousands + 9 tens + 2 ones + 6 tenths + 7 hundredths

62. _______________________________ 1 million + 3 hundred thousands + 8 ten thousands + 2 thousands + 9 tens + 6 ones + 3 tenths + 9 hundredths + 5 thousandths

Place Value: Expanded Notation

Provide the expanded notation for each value.

63. 8,236,737.543

64. 8,055,649.094

65. 2,493,351.750

66. 7,575,744.074

67. 7,122,870.583

68. 7,800,356.880

69. 2,911,239.395

70. 9,525,233.245

71. 7,783,266.892 ___________________________________

72. 5,800,008.303 ___________________________________

73. 1,312,494.303 ___________________________________

74. 4,202,274.290 ___________________________________

75. 5,471,071.900 _______________________

76. 9,612,371.301 _______________________

77. 3,273,574.577 _______________________

78. 5,667,698.595 _______________________

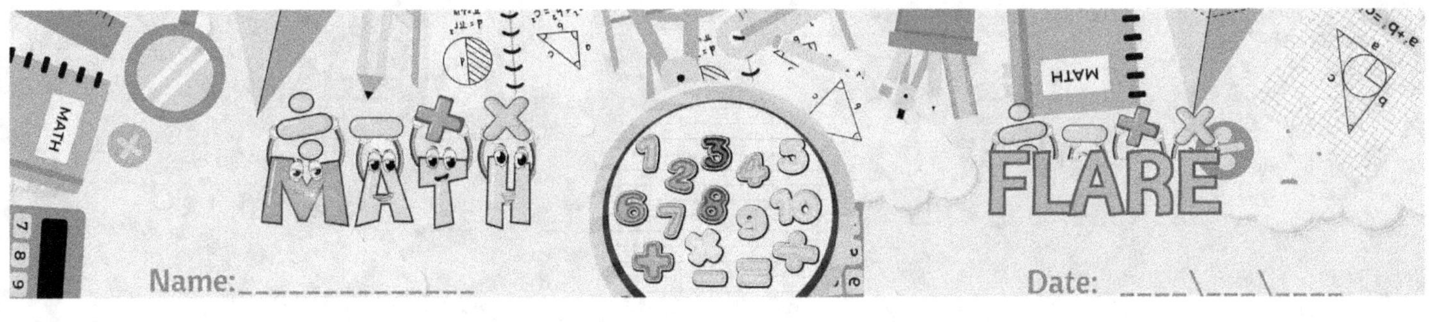

79. 1,699,956.163

80. 9,584,748.500

81. 3,273,644.767

82. 7,952,864.783

83. 4,739,588.214 _______________________________

84. 8,190,961.045 _______________________________

85. 7,113,943.014 _______________________________

86. 4,885,741.012 _______________________________

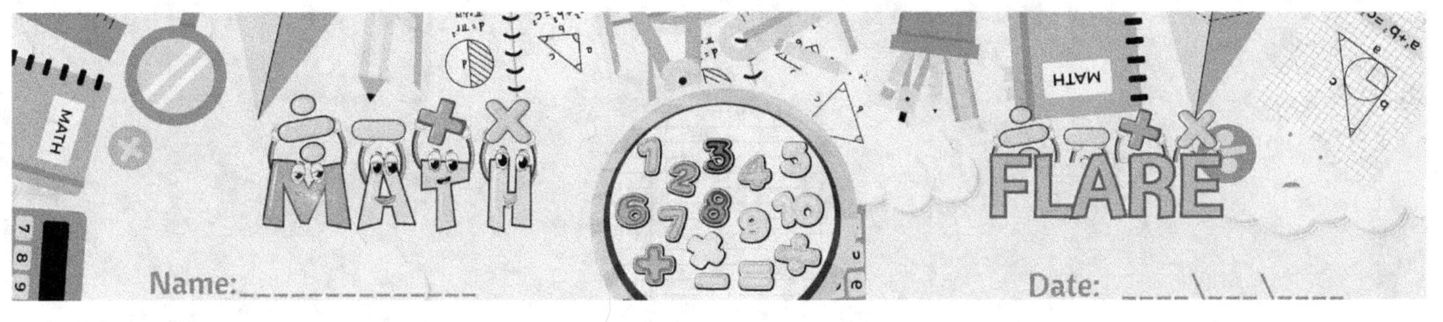

87. 6,514,806.436 _______________________________
____
____
____

88. 7,956,546.693 _______________________________
____
____
____

89. 5,086,299.951 _______________________________
____
____
____

90. 7,340,011.337 _______________________________
____
____
____

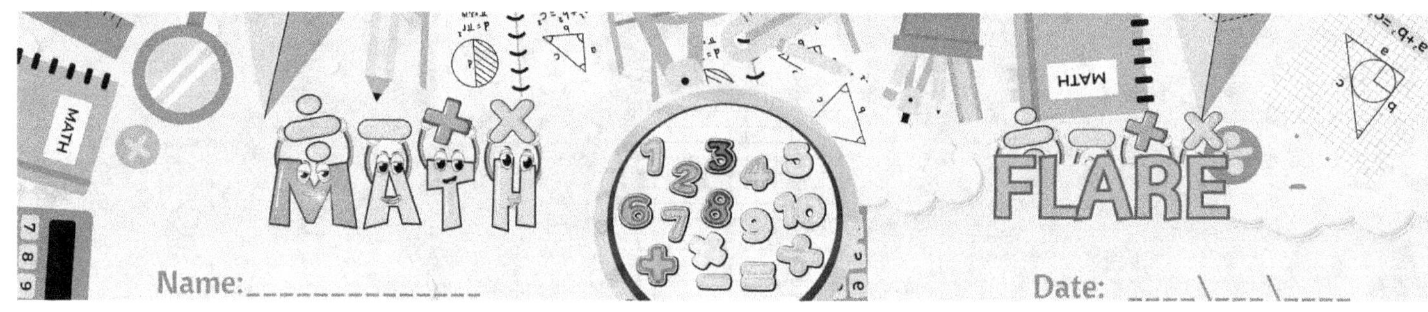

Place Value: Expanded Notation

Provide the expanded notation for each value.

91. _________________________________

2,000,000 + 60,000 + 900 + 30 + 7 + 0.6 + 0.03 + 0.008

92. _________________________________

9,000,000 + 100,000 + 60,000 + 6,000 + 300 + 20 + 3 + 0.8 + 0.09

93. _________________________________

3,000,000 + 700,000 + 10,000 + 4,000 + 50 + 6 + 0.9 + 0.02 + 0.009

94. _________________________________

5,000,000 + 500,000 + 70,000 + 1,000 + 200 + 20 + 8 + 0.05 + 0.007

95. _______________________________

$8{,}000{,}000 + 600{,}000 + 5{,}000 + 500 + 50 + 1 + 0.2 + 0.03 + 0.002$

96. _______________________________

$5{,}000{,}000 + 300{,}000 + 40{,}000 + 3{,}000 + 900 + 30 + 6 + 0.8 + 0.03 + 0.009$

97. _______________________________

$9{,}000{,}000 + 200{,}000 + 50{,}000 + 4{,}000 + 800 + 40 + 7 + 0.5 + 0.03 + 0.003$

98. _______________________________

$3{,}000{,}000 + 700{,}000 + 10{,}000 + 9{,}000 + 100 + 20 + 8 + 0.6 + 0.06 + 0.007$

99. _______________________________

$9{,}000{,}000 + 900{,}000 + 20{,}000 + 3{,}000 + 200 + 40 + 5 + 0.3 + 0.006$

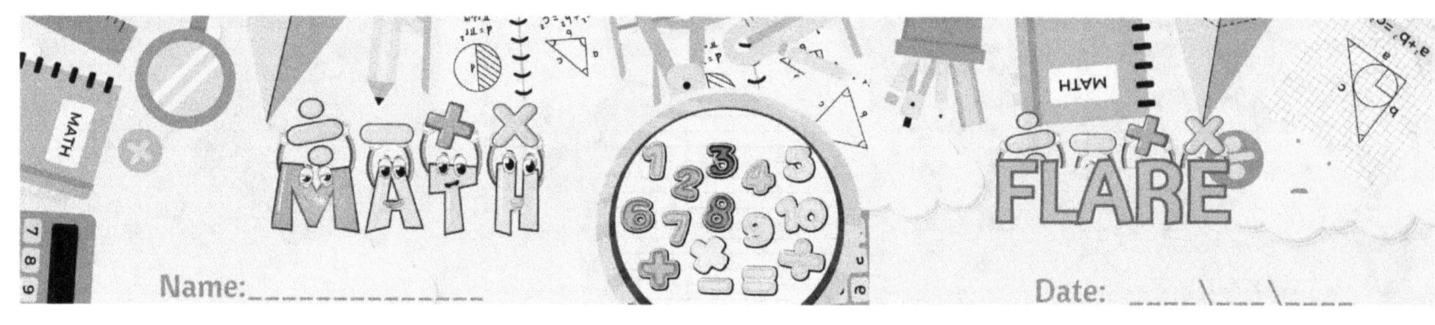

100. _______________________________
     6,000,000 + 500,000 + 30,000 + 1,000 + 600 + 80 + 0.2

101. _______________________________
     3,000,000 + 700,000 + 30,000 + 400 + 40 + 7 + 0.2 + 0.03 + 0.007

102. _______________________________
     3,000,000 + 800,000 + 90,000 + 9,000 + 100 + 70 + 2 + 0.4 + 0.04 + 0.006

103. _______________________________
     7,000,000 + 900,000 + 70,000 + 9,000 + 500 + 1 + 0.5 + 0.05 + 0.007

104. _______________________________
     3,000,000 + 600,000 + 40,000 + 4,000 + 30 + 5 + 0.2 + 0.06 + 0.004

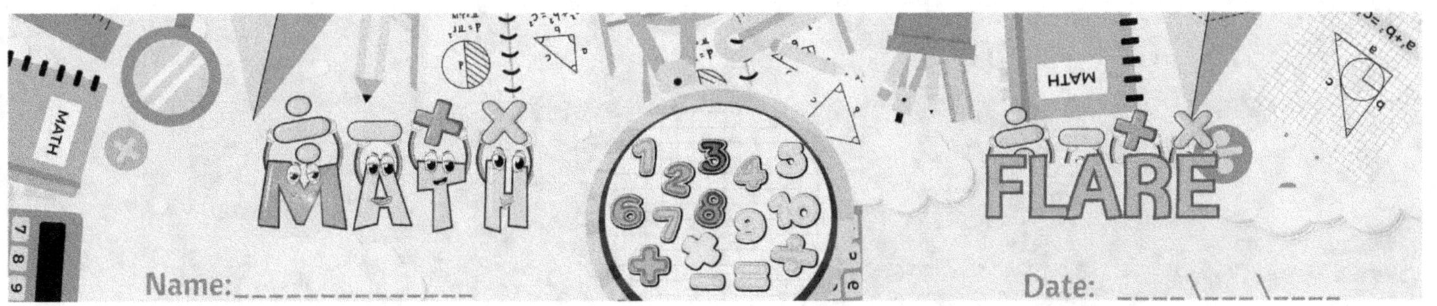

105. ___________________________

1,000,000 + 600,000 + 80,000 + 8,000 + 200 + 70 + 3 + 0.6 + 0.005

106. ___________________________

7,000,000 + 900,000 + 20,000 + 7,000 + 400 + 70 + 1 + 0.9 + 0.02

107. ___________________________

2,000,000 + 800,000 + 80,000 + 3,000 + 200 + 20 + 7 + 0.7 + 0.02 + 0.009

108. ___________________________

8,000,000 + 700,000 + 30,000 + 7,000 + 600 + 3 + 0.05

109. ___________________________

8,000,000 + 600,000 + 30,000 + 5,000 + 500 + 70 + 2 + 0.9 + 0.05 + 0.004

Name:________________ Date: ____________

110. _______________________________

$7,000,000 + 800,000 + 40,000 + 8,000 + 300 + 20 + 4 + 0.8 + 0.03 + 0.001$

111. _______________________________

$3,000,000 + 800,000 + 30,000 + 900 + 30 + 6 + 0.1 + 0.01 + 0.009$

112. _______________________________

$5,000,000 + 700,000 + 30,000 + 200 + 30 + 2 + 0.9 + 0.05 + 0.007$

113. _______________________________

$9,000,000 + 800,000 + 70,000 + 7,000 + 700 + 50 + 7 + 0.02 + 0.008$

114. _______________________________

$1,000,000 + 600,000 + 1,000 + 50 + 5 + 0.9 + 0.08 + 0.008$

Name:_________________________ Date: ____________

115. _________________________   2,000,000 + 700,000 + 60,000 + 8,000 + 1 + 0.5 + 0.01 + 0.007

116. _________________________   6,000,000 + 800,000 + 30,000 + 9,000 + 10 + 2 + 0.7 + 0.05 + 0.001

117. _________________________   8,000,000 + 600,000 + 60,000 + 5,000 + 500 + 10 + 3 + 0.2 + 0.03 + 0.008

118. _________________________   7,000,000 + 700,000 + 10,000 + 200 + 90 + 6 + 0.4 + 0.04 + 0.004

119. _________________________   6,000,000 + 30,000 + 2,000 + 700 + 20 + 0.9 + 0.05 + 0.002

Place Value: Expanded Notation

Provide the expanded notation for each value.

120. 5,324,515.018

121. 4,604,124.278

122. 4,982,504.971

123. 6,283,764.719

124. 4,871,577.376

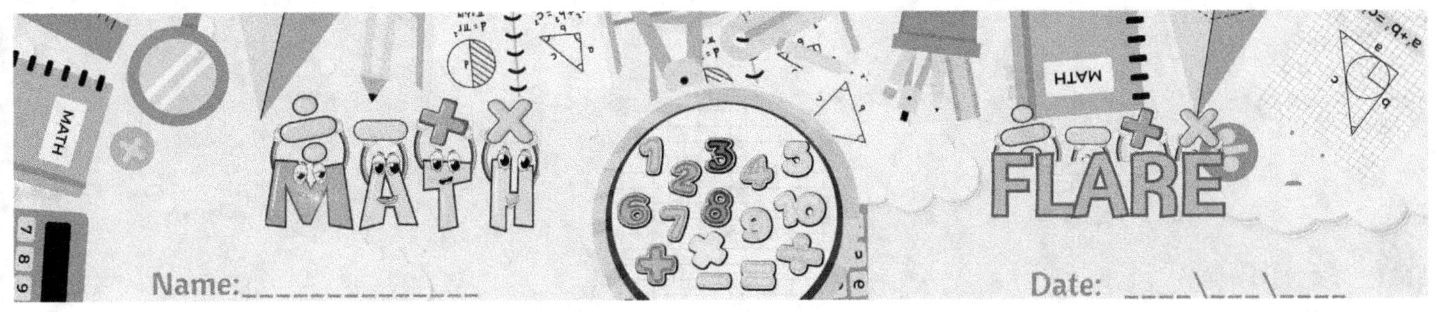

125. 5,335,254.898 ___________________________

126. 5,751,584.485 ___________________________

127. 7,998,186.584 ___________________________

128. 1,046,273.466 ___________________________

129. 6,277,884.726 ___________________________

130. 8,161,476.342 ___________________________

131. 9,371,155.793 ____________________________

132. 6,427,738.566 ____________________________

133. 4,021,061.001 ____________________________

134. 3,740,217.255 ____________________________

135. 8,564,844.058 ____________________________

136. 4,042,142.066 ____________________________

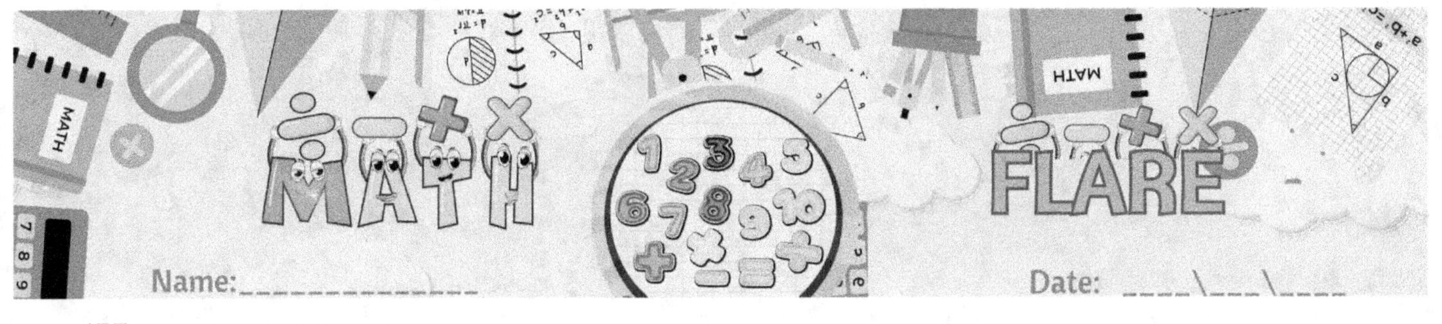

137. 1,725,074.342 _______________________________

138. 6,877,719.345 _______________________________

139. 8,243,733.431 _______________________________

140. 7,251,291.847 _______________________________

141. 4,622,502.611 _______________________________

142. 3,297,761.879 _______________________________

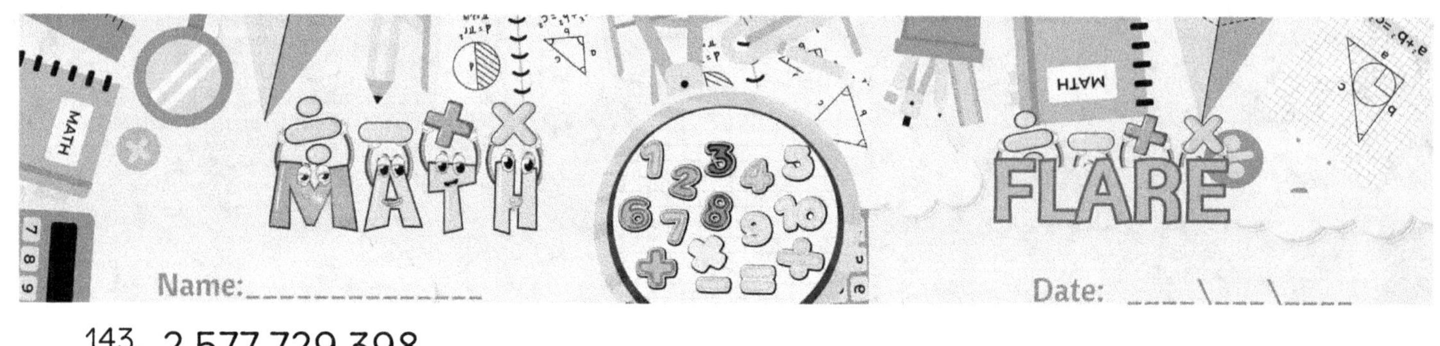

Name: _________________   Date: _______________

143. 2,577,729.398   ________________________
____

144. 1,525,093.737   ________________________
____

145. 4,753,917.978   ________________________
____

146. 6,272,560.805   ________________________
____

147. 3,578,955.163   ________________________
____

148. 1,137,602.473   ________________________
____

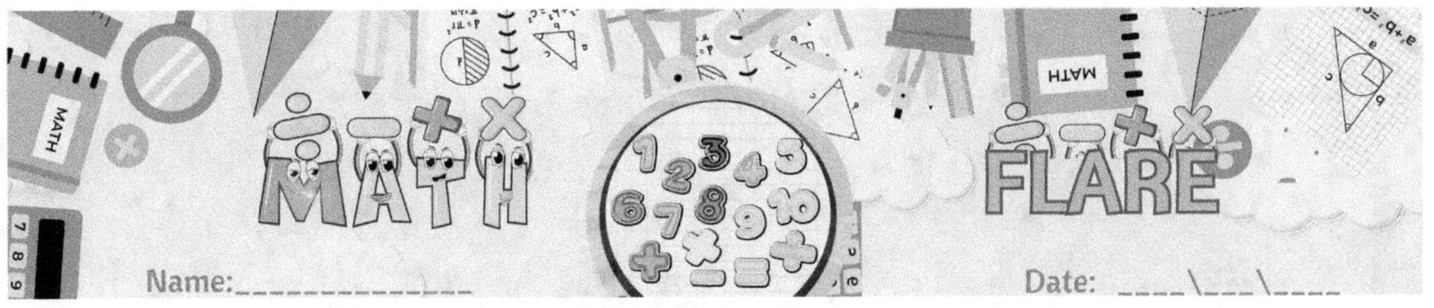

Place Value: Expanded Notation

Provide the expanded notation for each value.

149. _______________________________ five million three hundred eighty-six thousand three hundred eighty and nine hundred twenty-four thousandths

150. _______________________________ eight million one hundred thirty-five thousand four hundred seventeen and three hundred seventy thousandths

151. _______________________________ five million ninety-seven thousand seven hundred seventy-three and two hundred twenty-two thousandths

152. _______________________________ one million three hundred seventy-nine thousand two hundred eighty-seven and three hundred thirty thousandths

153. ______________________________ seven million eight hundred eighty-seven thousand one hundred twenty-three and nine hundred nineteen thousandths

154. ______________________________ two million four hundred six thousand three hundred five and fifteen thousandths

155. ______________________________ eight million four hundred thirty-six thousand three hundred thirty-two and six hundred eighty-nine thousandths

156. ______________________________ two million one hundred forty-two thousand nine hundred twenty-two and thirty-one thousandths

Name:__________________   Date: _______________

157. _________________________________ seven million seven hundred fifty-five thousand seven hundred fifty-nine and two hundred fifty thousandths

158. _________________________________ five million nine hundred ten thousand nine hundred forty-eight and three hundred nineteen thousandths

159. _________________________________ seven million six hundred seventy-five thousand two hundred eighty-four and six hundred six thousandths

160. _________________________________ three million three hundred sixty thousand one hundred twenty-three and thirty-seven thousandths

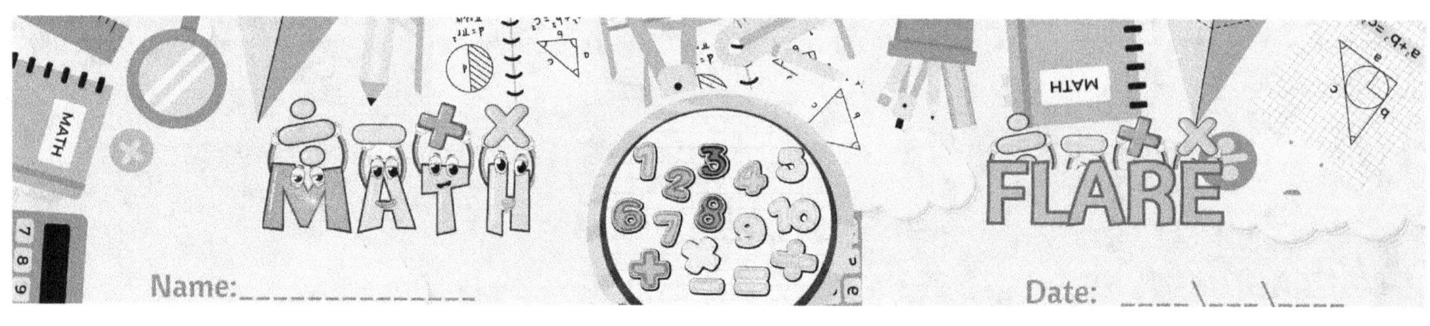

161. __________________________ eight million three hundred ninety-five thousand six hundred eighty-five and three hundred thirty-three thousandths

162. __________________________ seven million one hundred sixty-seven thousand four hundred twenty-nine and four hundred forty-seven thousandths

163. __________________________ one million five hundred ninety-nine thousand forty-five and six hundred eighty-nine thousandths

164. __________________________ two million one hundred sixty-one thousand six hundred eighty-three and eight hundred ninety-four thousandths

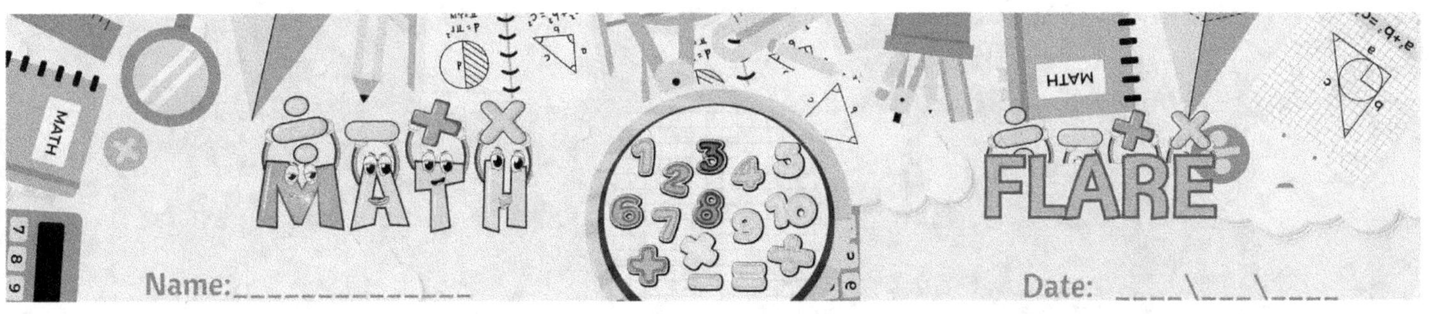

165. _______________________________ five million eighty thousand eight hundred ninety-two and one hundred thirty-six thousandth

166. _______________________________ seven million four hundred twenty-five thousand seven hundred five and fifty-seven thousandths

167. _______________________________ seven million two hundred seventy-two thousand nine hundred forty-six and four hundred fifty-two thousandths

168. _______________________________ two million three hundred seventy-five thousand seven hundred eighty-nine and one hundred seventy-five thousandth

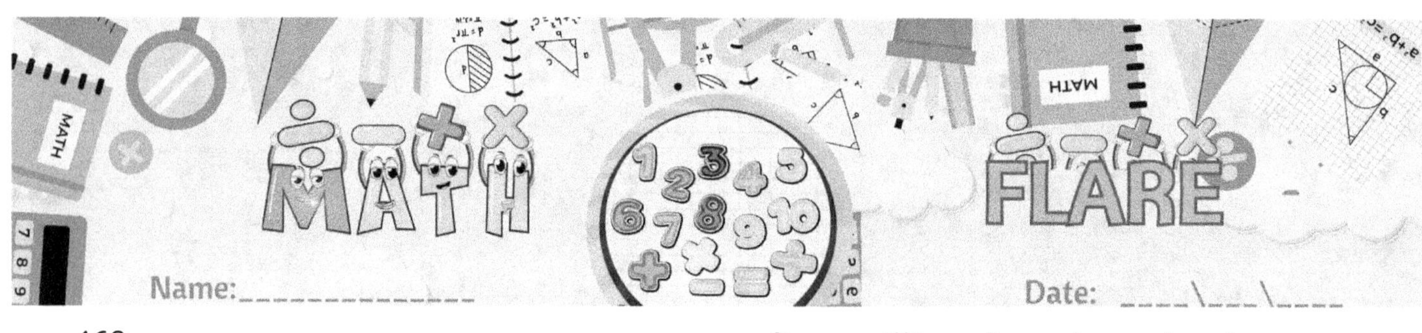

169. _________________________________ five million four hundred seventy-one thousand three hundred ninety-two and four hundred eighty-two thousandths

170. _________________________________ six million six hundred eighty-seven thousand six hundred fifty-eight and five hundred sixty-seven thousandths

171. _________________________________ one million four hundred twenty-three thousand three hundred seventy-two and two hundred thirty-four thousandths

172. _________________________________ seven million one hundred ninety-three thousand two hundred ninety-four and fifty-six thousandths

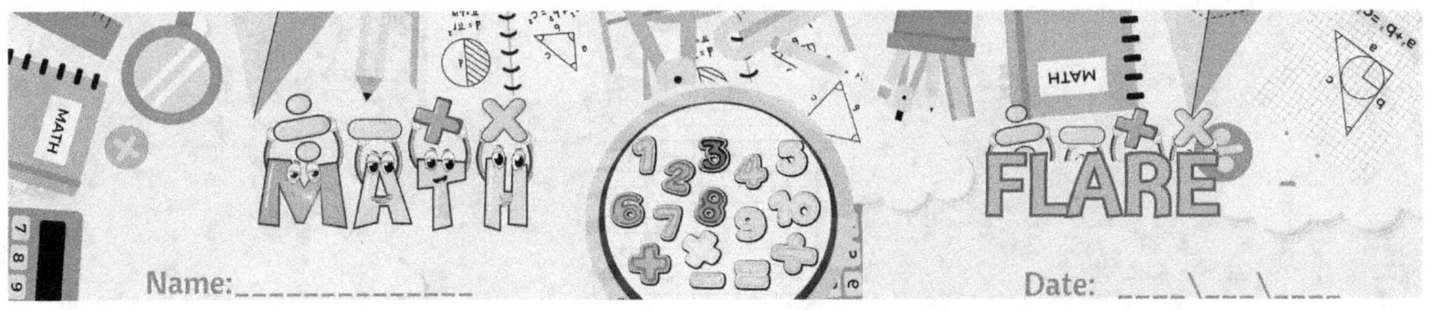

173. __________________________ nine million eight hundred thirteen thousand forty-two and one hundred thirty-one thousandth

174. __________________________ three million two hundred three thousand three hundred five and one hundred sixty-four thousandth

175. __________________________ one million seven hundred two thousand twelve and four hundred seven thousandths

176. __________________________ two million three hundred six thousand three hundred sixty-two and three hundred ninety-nine thousandths

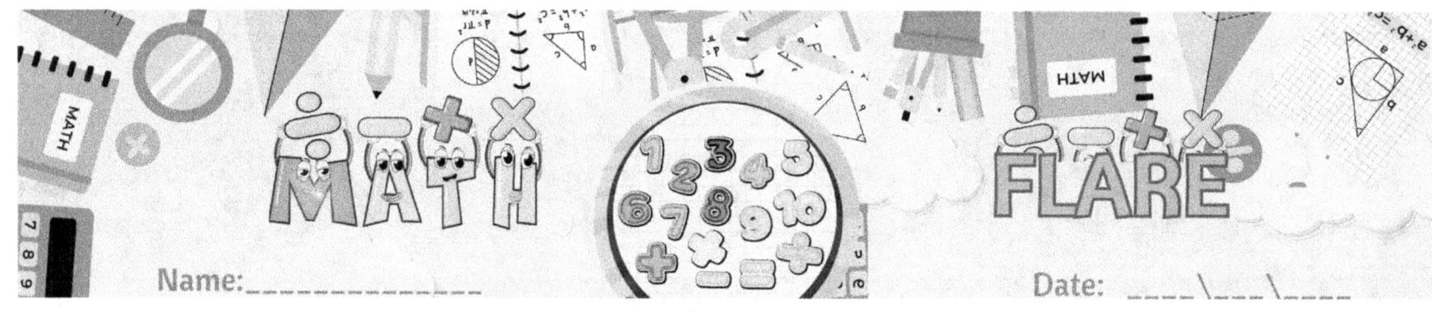

Place Value: Expanded Notation

Provide the expanded notation for each value.

177. 3,404,775.573

178. 5,758,670.982

179. 1,117,659.398

180. 9,062,694.091

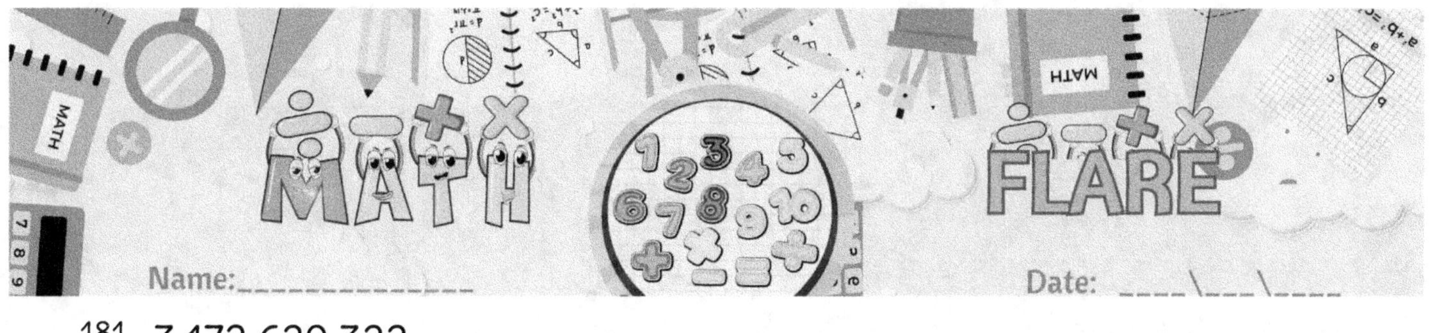

181. 3,172,629.322 _______________________________

182. 7,860,584.111 _______________________________

183. 5,659,892.541 _______________________________

184. 8,142,467.355 _______________________________

185. 4,063,703.120 _______________________________

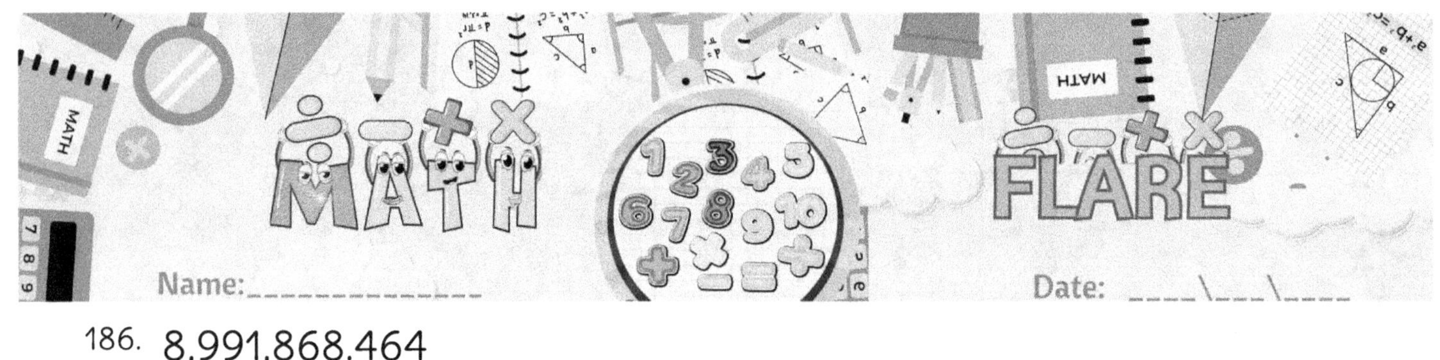

186. 8,991,868.464

187. 8,540,614.646

188. 2,614,755.986

189. 5,303,884.565

190. 7,421,922.028

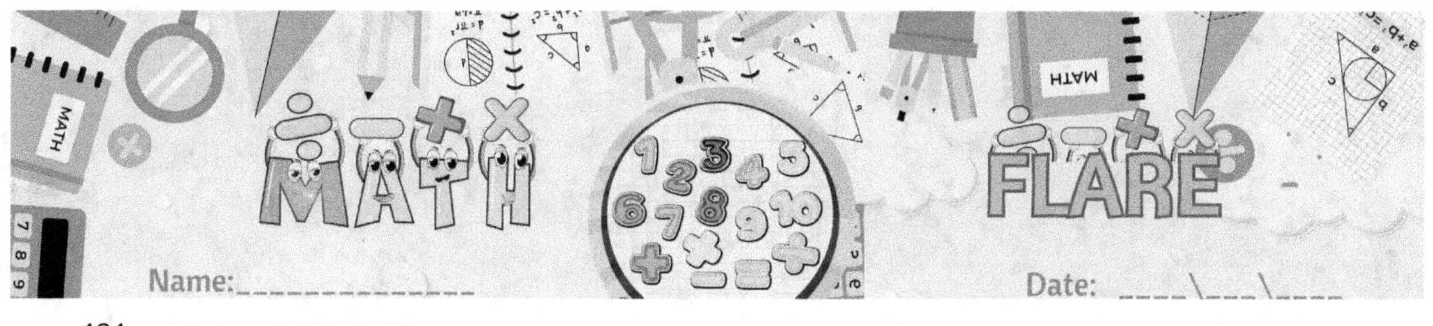

191. 6,286,382.815

192. 5,814,126.022

193. 9,202,434.738

194. 5,883,610.394

195. 8,855,606.513

196. 7,455,073.163 ______________________

197. 2,698,716.190 ______________________

198. 1,416,045.504 ______________________

199. 6,444,201.600 ______________________

200. 7,328,212.920 ______________________

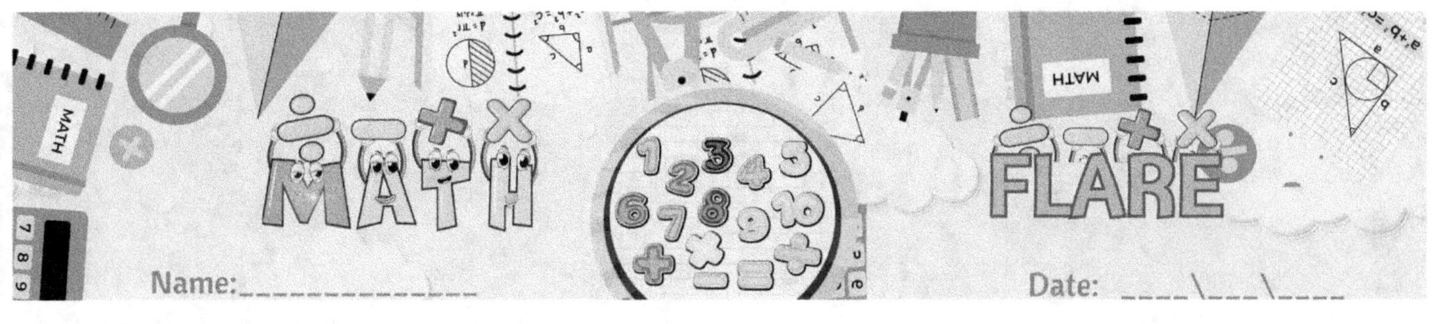

201. 8,999,614.352

202. 2,203,165.987

203. 5,666,209.990

204. 8,698,722.355

205. 7,712,045.135

206. 7,904,479.165

207. 1,566,245.198

208. 5,683,818.755

209. 1,704,292.608

210. 7,129,970.290

Rounding Numbers
Round to the underlined digit.

211. 1,889,023.488 = __________

212. 6,835,513.135 = __________

213. 7,376,825.662 = __________

214. 7,251,862.923 = __________

215. 4,262,718.235 = __________

216. 4,744,494.317 = __________

217. 7,317,550.108 = __________

218. 7,316,154.048 = __________

219. 9,806,441.193 = __________

220. 4,332,727.222 = __________

221. 7,186,378.797 = __________

222. 6,058,731.745 = __________

223. 6,441,626.361 = __________

224. 6,425,364.178 = __________

225. 4,446,030.23_9_ = __________   226. 3,4_3_0,108.576 = __________

227. 5,803,1_3_3.542 = __________   228. 5,208,1_4_7.736 = __________

229. 6,95_5_,294.102 = __________   230. _1_,784,489.924 = __________

231. 1,109,68_9_.960 = __________   232. 2,853,567.61_4_ = __________

233. _5_,418,785.621 = __________   234. 7,393,_2_63.123 = __________

235. 9,462,71_2_.256 = __________   236. 9,419,_8_05.629 = __________

237. 6,41_2_,900.213 = __________   238. _7_,163,900.012 = __________

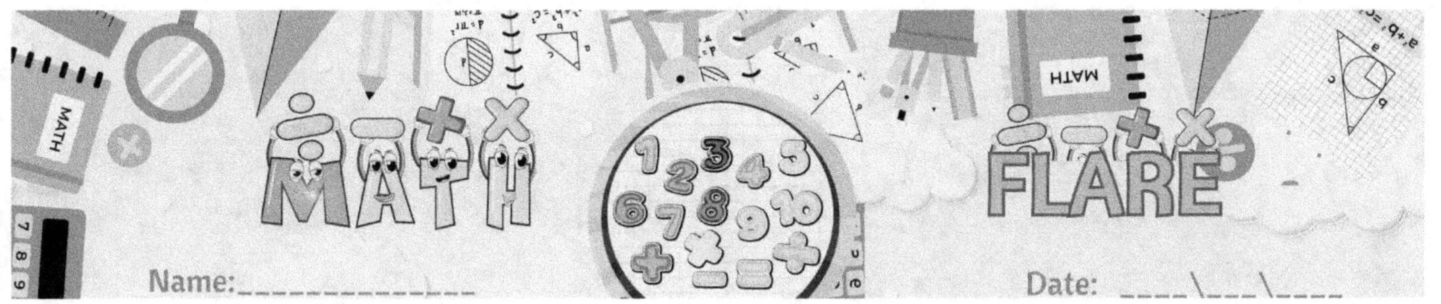

239. 8,127,673.682 = _____________   240. 2,261,415.479 = _____________

241. 3,941,018.939 = _____________   242. 6,108,544.952 = _____________

243. 5,480,188.921 = _____________   244. 4,348,793.222 = _____________

245. 7,769,898.247 = _____________   246. 2,668,589.962 = _____________

247. 9,564,384.771 = _____________   248. 5,321,462.572 = _____________

249. 3,332,829.872 = _____________   250. 3,544,866.683 = _____________

251. 1,646,792.886 = _____________   252. 2,797,829.282 = _____________

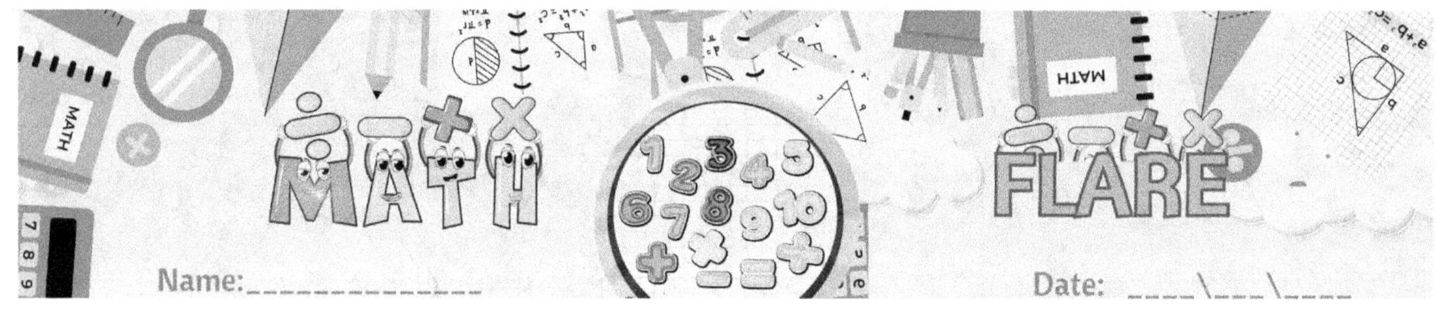

253. 1,304,158.731 = __________

254. 8,600,186.433 = __________

255. 3,265,025.233 = __________

256. 2,548,404.375 = __________

257. 1,734,735.387 = __________

258. 1,187,664.400 = __________

259. 1,472,873.990 = __________

260. 9,144,162.544 = __________

261. 3,978,212.071 = __________

262. 7,507,811.042 = __________

263. 9,439,263.245 = __________

264. 3,724,620.264 = __________

265. 1,803,768.163 = __________

266. 4,369,796.130 = __________

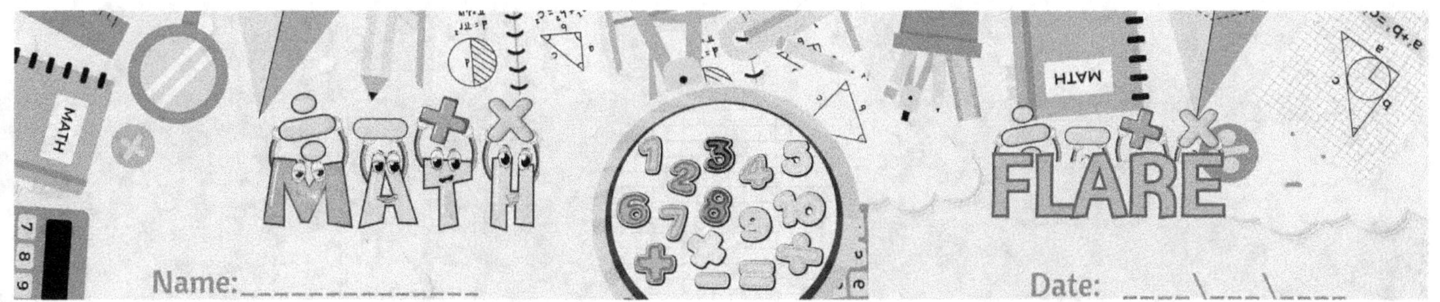

267. 6,326,994.146 = _____________

268. 8,689,976.766 = _____________

269. 4,193,492.101 = _____________

270. 4,234,595.143 = _____________

271. 2,131,221.238 = _____________

272. 5,623,599.630 = _____________

273. 6,091,671.615 = _____________

274. 7,075,554.941 = _____________

275. 1,016,379.484 = _____________

276. 1,132,085.865 = _____________

277. 3,290,217.734 = _____________

278. 6,136,408.996 = _____________

279. 4,639,843.847 = _____________

280. 3,898,913.785 = _____________

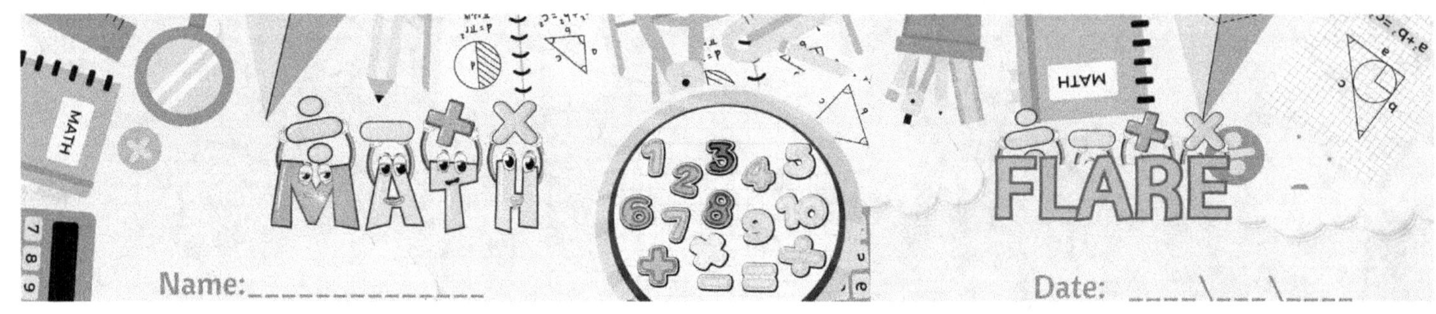

281. 7,4<u>1</u>6,483.275 = _____________

282. 8,874,1<u>3</u>4.643 = _____________

283. 5,1<u>3</u>5,725.604 = _____________

284. 2,7<u>5</u>6,439.126 = _____________

285. 3,<u>7</u>57,743.504 = _____________

286. 1,92<u>4</u>,876.476 = _____________

287. 5,<u>0</u>80,218.596 = _____________

288. 4,5<u>5</u>6,156.712 = _____________

289. 4,881,038.63<u>0</u> = _____________

290. 6,730,9<u>6</u>4.651 = _____________

291. 5,5<u>3</u>3,960.359 = _____________

292. 6,192,47<u>6</u>.846 = _____________

293. 6,4<u>2</u>6,854.292 = _____________

294. 4,403,075.6<u>6</u>8 = _____________

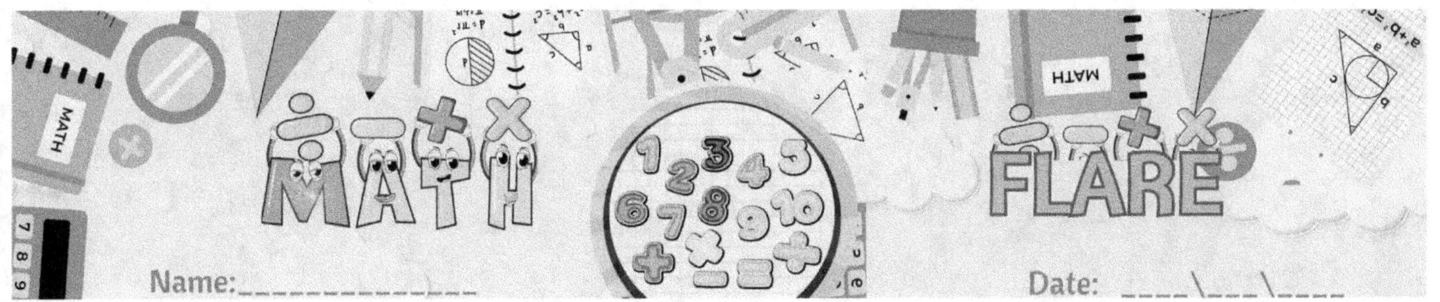

295. 7,0̲10,385.413 = __________

296. 8,15̲3,520.202 = __________

297. 9,871,454.1̲34 = __________

298. 7,922,602.1̲06 = __________

299. 5,796,755.77̲2 = __________

300. 5,128,650.9̲08 = __________

301. 2,828,717.56̲3 = __________

302. 5,35̲8,920.996 = __________

303. 9,278̲,217.519 = __________

304. 9,937,797.5̲35 = __________

305. 4,301,332.02̲0 = __________

306. 7̲,261,115.995 = __________

307. 4,244,228̲.364 = __________

308. 4,160̲,683.069 = __________

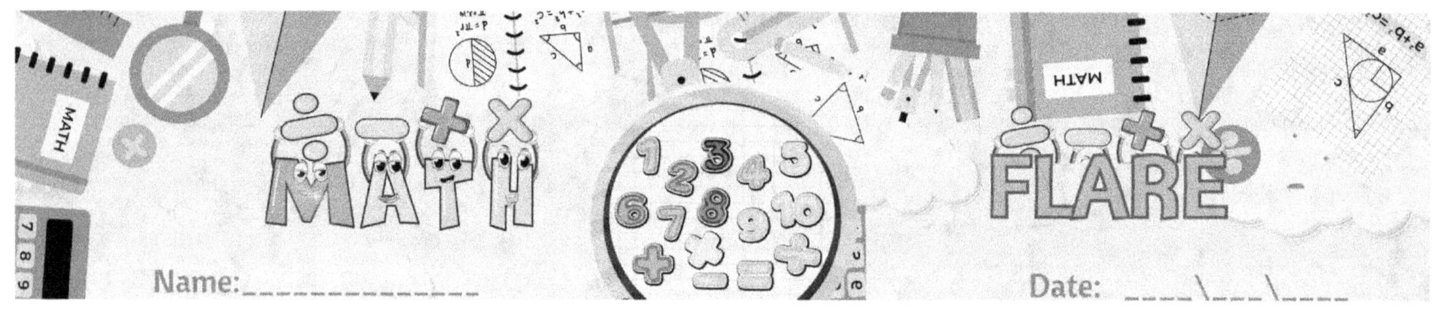

309. 7,198,853.257 = _____________

310. 1,279,230.783 = _____________

311. 2,452,035.304 = _____________

312. 2,577,555.562 = _____________

313. 1,240,780.147 = _____________

314. 7,831,051.933 = _____________

315. 6,882,475.056 = _____________

316. 4,510,565.881 = _____________

317. 4,114,783.620 = _____________

318. 4,025,388.993 = _____________

319. 1,249,034.767 = _____________

320. 2,322,456.647 = _____________

321. 9,413,982.461 = _____________

322. 5,168,173.392 = _____________

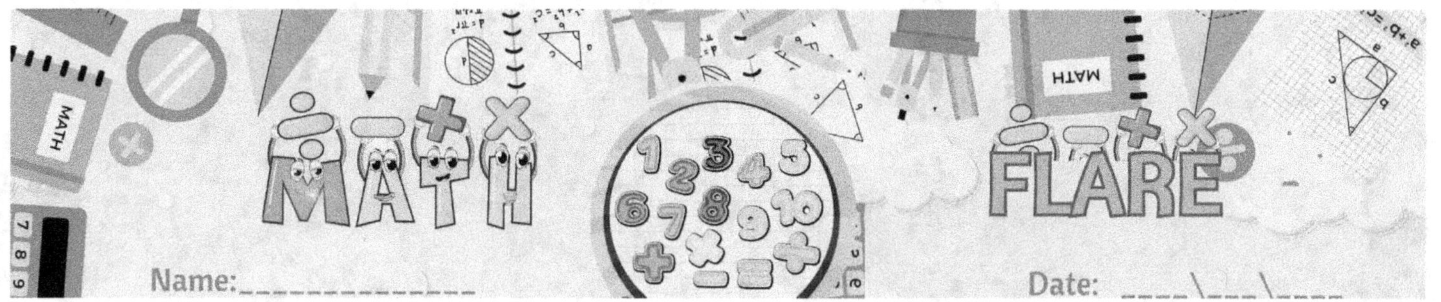

323. 1,286,706.145 = _____________

324. 9,974,070.720 = _____________

325. 2,379,268.646 = _____________

326. 2,541,037.877 = _____________

327. 8,638,283.771 = _____________

328. 8,784,525.338 = _____________

329. 6,910,058.404 = _____________

330. 2,381,298.986 = _____________

331. 5,598,527.861 = _____________

332. 2,602,665.514 = _____________

333. 3,318,521.460 = _____________

334. 3,281,625.697 = _____________

335. 5,019,418.235 = _____________

336. 2,559,492.745 = _____________

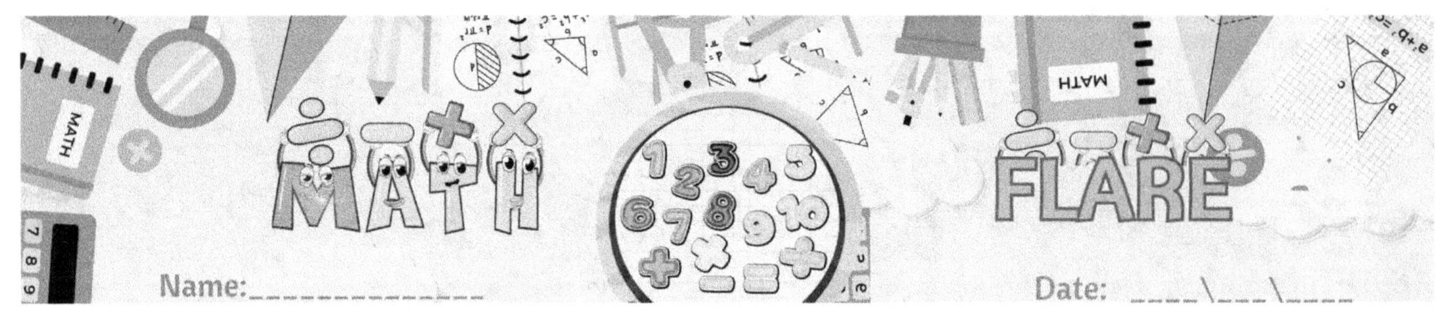

337. 6,951,003.829 = _____________

338. 6,369,963.143 = _____________

339. 9,118,760.319 = _____________

340. 5,923,215.218 = _____________

341. 7,732,506.669 = _____________

342. 8,160,998.234 = _____________

343. 4,275,227.702 = _____________

344. 7,325,240.303 = _____________

345. 7,709,878.669 = _____________

346. 1,136,287.990 = _____________

347. 3,189,098.727 = _____________

348. 8,398,746.635 = _____________

349. 4,315,269.583 = _____________

350. 7,862,776.611 = _____________

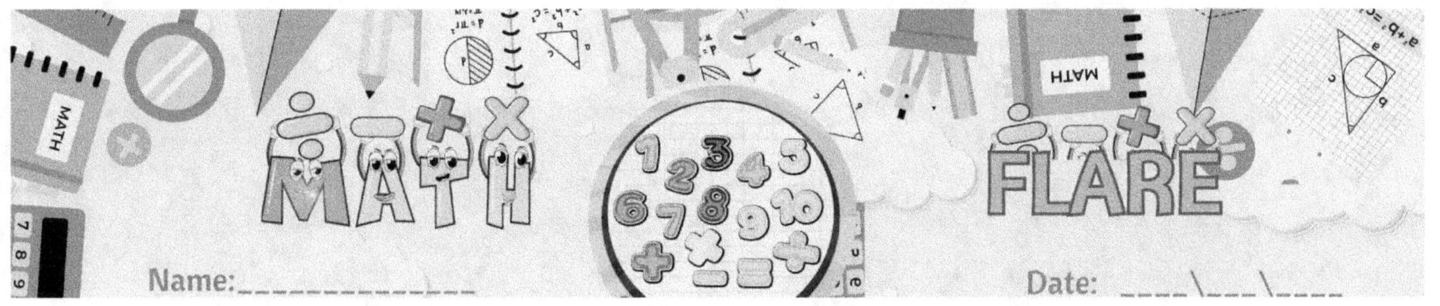

351. 9,475,4<u>8</u>5.187 = _____________

352. <u>7</u>,807,228.670 = _____________

353. 4,554,5<u>8</u>1.849 = _____________

354. 1,572,291.<u>4</u>67 = _____________

355. 3,<u>9</u>74,742.160 = _____________

356. 9,423,023.5<u>3</u>0 = _____________

357. 4,2<u>2</u>5,784.414 = _____________

358. 4,839,133.4<u>6</u>0 = _____________

359. 3,236,5<u>3</u>2.420 = _____________

360. 5,209,838.73<u>9</u> = _____________

361. <u>4</u>,972,351.615 = _____________

362. 1,039,94<u>5</u>.686 = _____________

363. 6,<u>9</u>78,048.685 = _____________

364. 1,439,356.8<u>1</u>7 = _____________

ANSWERS

Page 1:   Place Value

1. 6 hundred thousands
2. 6 hundreds
3. 8 ten thousands
4. 4 millions
5. 7 hundreds
6. 1 ten million
7. 0 hundredths
8. 4 tenths
9. 9 hundred thousands
10. 2 hundred millions
11. 1 thousand
12. 9 ones
13. 0 hundreds
14. 9 hundredths
15. 5 hundreds
16. 7 millions
17. 6 tenths
18. 2 ten millions
19. 2 thousandths
20. 2 tens
21. 5 tens
22. 0 hundred thousands
23. 5 hundred thousands
24. 8 thousands
25. 8 thousands
26. 5 ten thousands
27. 9 ones
28. 6 ones
29. 9 ten thousands
30. 4 ten millions

Page 5:   Place Value: Expanded Notation

31. 1,596,441.930
32. 9,638,269.735
33. 7,466,261.189
34. 7,940,338.326
35. 2,111,745.047
36. 1,914,764.719
37. 8,833,844.330
38. 2,689,310.102
39. 1,496,628.421

40. 3,425,600.273

41. 7,193,563.064

42. 4,425,111.331

43. 4,759,893.764

44. 1,325,911.077

45. 3,310,822.062

46. 8,373,084.005

47. 4,392,187.957

48. 2,437,707.447

49. 6,497,314.674

50. 5,709,203.705

51. 7,514,279.905

52. 1,038,188.328

53. 3,072,372.217

54. 6,090,103.252

55. 6,501,659.236

56. 6,458,321.842

57. 9,655,498.100

58. 3,210,941.208

59. 2,643,421.613

60. 1,599,947.766

61. 5,699,092.670

62. 1,382,096.395

Page 13: Place Value: Expanded Notation

63. 8 millions + 2 hundred thousands + 3 ten thousands + 6 thousands + 7 hundreds + 3 tens + 7 ones + 5 tenths + 4 hundredths + 3 thousandths

64. 8 millions + 5 ten thousands + 5 thousands + 6 hundreds + 4 tens + 9 ones + 9 hundredths + 4 thousandths

65. 2 millions + 4 hundred thousands + 9 ten thousands + 3 thousands + 3 hundreds + 5 tens + 1 one + 7 tenths + 5 hundredths

66. 7 millions + 5 hundred thousands + 7 ten thousands + 5 thousands + 7 hundreds + 4 tens + 4 ones + 7 hundredths + 4 thousandths

67. 7 millions + 1 hundred thousand + 2 ten thousands + 2 thousands + 8 hundreds + 7 tens + 5 tenths + 8 hundredths + 3 thousandths

68. 7 millions + 8 hundred thousands + 3 hundreds + 5 tens + 6 ones + 8 tenths + 8 hundredths

69. 2 millions + 9 hundred thousands + 1 ten thousand + 1 thousand + 2 hundreds + 3 tens + 9 ones + 3 tenths + 9 hundredths + 5 thousandths

70. 9 millions + 5 hundred thousands + 2 ten thousands + 5 thousands + 2 hundreds + 3 tens + 3 ones + 2 tenths + 4 hundredths + 5 thousandths

71. 7 millions + 7 hundred thousands + 8 ten thousands + 3 thousands + 2 hundreds + 6 tens + 6 ones + 8 tenths + 9 hundredths + 2 thousandths

72. 5 millions + 8 hundred thousands + 8 ones + 3 tenths + 3 thousandths

73. 1 million + 3 hundred thousands + 1 ten thousand + 2 thousands + 4 hundreds + 9 tens + 4 ones + 3 tenths + 3 thousandths

74. 4 millions + 2 hundred thousands + 2 thousands + 2 hundreds + 7 tens + 4 ones + 2 tenths + 9 hundredths

75. 5 millions + 4 hundred thousands + 7 ten thousands + 1 thousand + 7 tens + 1 one + 9 tenths

76. 9 millions + 6 hundred thousands + 1 ten thousand + 2 thousands + 3 hundreds + 7 tens + 1 one + 3 tenths + 1 thousandth

77. 3 millions + 2 hundred thousands + 7 ten thousands + 3 thousands + 5 hundreds + 7 tens + 4 ones + 5 tenths + 7 hundredths + 7 thousandths

78. 5 millions + 6 hundred thousands + 6 ten thousands + 7 thousands + 6 hundreds + 9 tens + 8 ones + 5 tenths + 9 hundredths + 5 thousandths

79. 1 million + 6 hundred thousands + 9 ten thousands + 9 thousands + 9 hundreds + 5 tens + 6 ones + 1 tenth + 6 hundredths + 3 thousandths

80. 9 millions + 5 hundred thousands + 8 ten thousands + 4 thousands + 7 hundreds + 4 tens + 8 ones + 5 tenths

81. 3 millions + 2 hundred thousands + 7 ten thousands + 3 thousands + 6 hundreds + 4 tens + 4 ones + 7 tenths + 6 hundredths + 7 thousandths

82. 7 millions + 9 hundred thousands + 5 ten thousands + 2 thousands + 8 hundreds + 6 tens + 4 ones + 7 tenths + 8 hundredths + 3 thousandths

83. 4 millions + 7 hundred thousands + 3 ten thousands + 9 thousands + 5 hundreds + 8 tens + 8 ones + 2 tenths + 1 hundredth + 4 thousandths

84. 8 millions + 1 hundred thousand + 9 ten thousands + 9 hundreds + 6 tens + 1 one + 4 hundredths + 5 thousandths

85. 7 millions + 1 hundred thousand + 1 ten thousand + 3 thousands + 9 hundreds + 4 tens + 3 ones + 1 hundredth + 4 thousandths

86. 4 millions + 8 hundred thousands + 8 ten thousands + 5 thousands + 7 hundreds + 4 tens + 1 one + 1 hundredth + 2 thousandths

87. 6 millions + 5 hundred thousands + 1 ten thousand + 4 thousands + 8 hundreds + 6 ones + 4 tenths + 3 hundredths + 6 thousandths

88. 7 millions + 9 hundred thousands + 5 ten thousands + 6 thousands + 5 hundreds + 4 tens + 6 ones + 6 tenths + 9 hundredths + 3 thousandths

89. 5 millions + 8 ten thousands + 6 thousands + 2 hundreds + 9 tens + 9 ones + 9 tenths + 5 hundredths + 1 thousandth

90. 7 millions + 3 hundred thousands + 4 ten thousands + 1 ten + 1 one + 3 tenths + 3 hundredths + 7 thousandths

Page 20:   Place Value: Expanded Notation

91. 2,060,937.638	92. 9,166,323.890	93. 3,714,056.929
94. 5,571,228.057	95. 8,605,551.232	96. 5,343,936.839
97. 9,254,847.533	98. 3,719,128.667	99. 9,923,245.306
100. 6,531,680.200	101. 3,730,447.237	102. 3,899,172.446
103. 7,979,501.557	104. 3,644,035.264	105. 1,688,273.605
106. 7,927,471.920	107. 2,883,227.729	108. 8,737,603.050
109. 8,635,572.954	110. 7,848,324.831	111. 3,830,936.119

112. 5,730,232.957   113. 9,877,757.028   114. 1,601,055.988

115. 2,768,001.517   116. 6,839,012.751   117. 8,665,513.238

118. 7,710,296.444   119. 6,032,720.952

Page 26: Place Value: Expanded Notation

120. 5,000,000 + 300,000 + 20,000 + 4,000 + 500 + 10 + 5 + 0.01 + 0.008

121. 4,000,000 + 600,000 + 4,000 + 100 + 20 + 4 + 0.2 + 0.07 + 0.008

122. 4,000,000 + 900,000 + 80,000 + 2,000 + 500 + 4 + 0.9 + 0.07 + 0.001

123. 6,000,000 + 200,000 + 80,000 + 3,000 + 700 + 60 + 4 + 0.7 + 0.01 + 0.009

124. 4,000,000 + 800,000 + 70,000 + 1,000 + 500 + 70 + 7 + 0.3 + 0.07 + 0.006

125. 5,000,000 + 300,000 + 30,000 + 5,000 + 200 + 50 + 4 + 0.8 + 0.09 + 0.008

126. 5,000,000 + 700,000 + 50,000 + 1,000 + 500 + 80 + 4 + 0.4 + 0.08 + 0.005

127. 7,000,000 + 900,000 + 90,000 + 8,000 + 100 + 80 + 6 + 0.5 + 0.08 + 0.004

128. 1,000,000 + 40,000 + 6,000 + 200 + 70 + 3 + 0.4 + 0.06 + 0.006

129. 6,000,000 + 200,000 + 70,000 + 7,000 + 800 + 80 + 4 + 0.7 + 0.02 + 0.006

130. 8,000,000 + 100,000 + 60,000 + 1,000 + 400 + 70 + 6 + 0.3 + 0.04 + 0.002

131. 9,000,000 + 300,000 + 70,000 + 1,000 + 100 + 50 + 5 + 0.7 + 0.09 + 0.003

132. 6,000,000 + 400,000 + 20,000 + 7,000 + 700 + 30 + 8 + 0.5 + 0.06 + 0.006

133. 4,000,000 + 20,000 + 1,000 + 60 + 1 + 0.001

134. 3,000,000 + 700,000 + 40,000 + 200 + 10 + 7 + 0.2 + 0.05 + 0.005

135. 8,000,000 + 500,000 + 60,000 + 4,000 + 800 + 40 + 4 + 0.05 + 0.008

136. 4,000,000 + 40,000 + 2,000 + 100 + 40 + 2 + 0.06 + 0.006

137. 1,000,000 + 700,000 + 20,000 + 5,000 + 70 + 4 + 0.3 + 0.04 + 0.002

138. 6,000,000 + 800,000 + 70,000 + 7,000 + 700 + 10 + 9 + 0.3 + 0.04 + 0.005

139. 8,000,000 + 200,000 + 40,000 + 3,000 + 700 + 30 + 3 + 0.4 + 0.03 + 0.001

140. 7,000,000 + 200,000 + 50,000 + 1,000 + 200 + 90 + 1 + 0.8 + 0.04 + 0.007

141. 4,000,000 + 600,000 + 20,000 + 2,000 + 500 + 2 + 0.6 + 0.01 + 0.001

142. 3,000,000 + 200,000 + 90,000 + 7,000 + 700 + 60 + 1 + 0.8 + 0.07 + 0.009

143. 2,000,000 + 500,000 + 70,000 + 7,000 + 700 + 20 + 9 + 0.3 + 0.09 + 0.008

144. 1,000,000 + 500,000 + 20,000 + 5,000 + 90 + 3 + 0.7 + 0.03 + 0.007

145. 4,000,000 + 700,000 + 50,000 + 3,000 + 900 + 10 + 7 + 0.9 + 0.07 + 0.008

146. 6,000,000 + 200,000 + 70,000 + 2,000 + 500 + 60 + 0.8 + 0.005

147. 3,000,000 + 500,000 + 70,000 + 8,000 + 900 + 50 + 5 + 0.1 + 0.06 + 0.003

148. 1,000,000 + 100,000 + 30,000 + 7,000 + 600 + 2 + 0.4 + 0.07 + 0.003

Page 31: Place Value: Expanded Notation

149. 5,386,380.924	150. 8,135,417.370	151. 5,097,773.222
152. 1,379,287.330	153. 7,887,123.919	154. 2,406,305.015
155. 8,436,332.689	156. 2,142,922.031	157. 7,755,759.250
158. 5,910,948.319	159. 7,675,284.606	160. 3,360,123.037
161. 8,395,685.333	162. 7,167,429.447	163. 1,599,045.689
164. 2,161,683.894	165. 5,080,892.136	166. 7,425,705.057
167. 7,272,946.452	168. 2,375,789.175	169. 5,471,392.482
170. 6,687,658.567	171. 1,423,372.234	172. 7,193,294.056
173. 9,813,042.131	174. 3,203,305.164	175. 1,702,012.407

176. 2,306,362.399

Page 38: Place Value: Expanded Notation

177. three million four hundred four thousand seven hundred seventy-five and five hundred seventy-three thousandths

178. five million seven hundred fifty-eight thousand six hundred seventy and nine hundred eighty-two thousandths

179. one million one hundred seventeen thousand six hundred fifty-nine and three hundred ninety-eight thousandths

180. nine million sixty-two thousand six hundred ninety-four and ninety-one thousandths

181. three million one hundred seventy-two thousand six hundred twenty-nine and three hundred twenty-two thousandths

182. seven million eight hundred sixty thousand five hundred eighty-four and one hundred eleven thousandth

183. five million six hundred fifty-nine thousand eight hundred ninety-two and five hundred forty-one thousandths

184. eight million one hundred forty-two thousand four hundred sixty-seven and three hundred fifty-five thousandths

185. four million sixty-three thousand seven hundred three and one hundred twenty thousandth

186. eight million nine hundred ninety-one thousand eight hundred sixty-eight and four hundred sixty-four thousandths

187. eight million five hundred forty thousand six hundred fourteen and six hundred forty-six thousandths

188. two million six hundred fourteen thousand seven hundred fifty-five and nine hundred eighty-six thousandths

189. five million three hundred three thousand eight hundred eighty-four and five hundred sixty-five thousandths

190. seven million four hundred twenty-one thousand nine hundred twenty-two and twenty-eight thousandths

191. six million two hundred eighty-six thousand three hundred eighty-two and eight hundred fifteen thousandths

192. five million eight hundred fourteen thousand one hundred twenty-six and twenty-two thousandths

193. nine million two hundred two thousand four hundred thirty-four and seven hundred thirty-eight thousandths

194. five million eight hundred eighty-three thousand six hundred ten and three hundred ninety-four thousandths

195. eight million eight hundred fifty-five thousand six hundred six and five hundred thirteen thousandths

196. seven million four hundred fifty-five thousand seventy-three and one hundred sixty-three thousandth

197. two million six hundred ninety-eight thousand seven hundred sixteen and one hundred ninety thousandth

198. one million four hundred sixteen thousand forty-five and five hundred four thousandths

199. six million four hundred forty-four thousand two hundred one and six hundred thousandths

200. seven million three hundred twenty-eight thousand two hundred twelve and nine hundred twenty thousandths

201. eight million nine hundred ninety-nine thousand six hundred fourteen and three hundred fifty-two thousandths

202. two million two hundred three thousand one hundred sixty-five and nine hundred eighty-seven thousandths

203. five million six hundred sixty-six thousand two hundred nine and nine hundred ninety thousandths

204. eight million six hundred ninety-eight thousand seven hundred twenty-two and three hundred fifty-five thousandths

205. seven million seven hundred twelve thousand forty-five and one hundred thirty-five thousandth

206. seven million nine hundred four thousand four hundred seventy-nine and one hundred sixty-five thousandth

207. one million five hundred sixty-six thousand two hundred forty-five and one hundred ninety-eight thousandth

208. five million six hundred eighty-three thousand eight hundred eighteen and seven hundred fifty-five thousandths

209. one million seven hundred four thousand two hundred ninety-two and six hundred eight thousandths

210. seven million one hundred twenty-nine thousand nine hundred seventy and two hundred ninety thousandths

Page 45: Rounding Numbers

211. 1,889,023.488	212. 6,835,513	213. 7,400,000
214. 7,252,000	215. 4,262,718	216. 4,744,494.317
217. 7,317,600	218. 7,300,000	219. 9,806,441.2
220. 4,330,000	221. 7,186,400	222. 6,058,732
223. 6,441,626	224. 6,425,364.18	225. 4,446,030.239
226. 3,430,000	227. 5,803,130	228. 5,208,100
229. 6,955,000	230. 2,000,000	231. 1,109,690
232. 2,853,567.614	233. 5,000,000	234. 7,393,300
235. 9,462,712	236. 9,419,800	237. 6,413,000
238. 7,000,000	239. 8,128,000	240. 2,261,415
241. 3,900,000	242. 6,000,000	243. 5,480,190
244. 4,348,793.222	245. 7,770,000	246. 3,000,000

247. 9,564,384.771

248. 5,320,000

249. 3,332,829.9

250. 3,545,000

251. 2,000,000

252. 3,000,000

253. 1,304,158.7

254. 8,600,186.43

255. 3,265,000

256. 2,548,000

257. 1,700,000

258. 1,187,660

259. 1,500,000

260. 9,144,000

261. 3,978,210

262. 7,508,000

263. 9,439,263.25

264. 3,724,620.3

265. 1,800,000

266. 4,400,000

267. 6,327,000

268. 8,700,000

269. 4,193,492.101

270. 4,234,595

271. 2,131,221.238

272. 5,624,000

273. 6,090,000

274. 7,075,555

275. 1,000,000

276. 1,130,000

277. 3,290,200

278. 6,000,000

279. 4,639,844

280. 3,898,913.785

281. 7,420,000

282. 8,874,100

283. 5,140,000

284. 2,760,000

285. 3,800,000

286. 1,925,000

287. 5,100,000

288. 4,600,000

289. 4,881,038.63

290. 6,731,000

291. 5,530,000

292. 6,192,477

293. 6,430,000

294. 4,403,075.67

295. 7,000,000

296. 8,150,000

297. 9,871,454.1

298. 7,922,602.1

299. 5,796,755.77

300. 5,128,650.9

301. 2,828,717.56

302. 5,360,000

303. 9,278,000

304. 9,937,797.5

305. 4,301,332.02

306. 7,000,000

307. 4,244,228

308. 4,161,000

309. 7,198,853

310. 1,279,200

311. 2,452,000

312. 2,578,000

313. 1,240,000

314. 7,831,051.933

315. 6,882,480

316. 4,511,000

317. 4,000,000

318. 4,025,389

319. 1,200,000

320. 2,300,000

321. 9,413,982

322. 5,168,173.4

323. 1,287,000

324. 9,974,070

325. 2,380,000

326. 2,540,000

327. 9,000,000

328. 8,784,525.3

329. 6,910,058.4

330. 2,381,000

331. 5,598,527.86

332. 3,000,000

333. 3,318,500

334. 3,000,000

335. 5,019,418.24

336. 2,559,500

337. 6,951,000

338. 6,400,000

339. 9,118,800

340. 5,923,215.22

341. 7,700,000

342. 8,160,998.23

343. 4,300,000

344. 7,325,240.303

345. 7,709,878.67

346. 1,136,288

347. 3,189,098.73

348. 8,398,747

349. 4,315,269.583

350. 7,862,780

351. 9,475,490

352. 8,000,000

353. 4,554,580

354. 1,572,291.5

355. 4,000,000

356. 9,423,023.5

357. 4,230,000

358. 4,839,133.46

359. 3,236,530

360. 5,209,838.739

361. 5,000,000

362. 1,039,946

363. 7,000,000

364. 1,439,356.82